i explore

DINOSAURS

3-D

Throughout this book, you will find 3-D pictures to explore. Look for the 3-D glasses symbol to find them! To view the pictures, remove the 3-D glasses from the book cover and then hold the red lens over your left eye and the blue lens over your right eye. Watch as the picture comes to life!

i explore

DINOSAURS

make
believe
ideas

Written by Sarah Creese.
With thanks to Professor Mike Benton.

Copyright © 2012 make believe ideas ltd
The Wilderness, Berkhamsted, Hertfordshire, HP4 2AZ, UK.
565 Royal Parkway, Nashville, TN 37214, USA.

www.makebelieveideas.com

Reading together

This book is an ideal first reader for your child, combining simple words and sentences with stunning color photography. Here are some of the many ways you can help your child take those first steps in reading. Encourage your child to:

- Look at and explore the detail in the pictures.
- Sound out the letters in each word.
- Read and repeat each short sentence.

Look at the pictures

Make the most of each page by talking about the pictures and finding key words. Here are some questions you can use to discuss each page as you go along:

- Can you describe this dinosaur?
- How do you feel about this dinosaur? What do you like or dislike about it?
- What questions do you have about this dinosaur?

Sound out the words

Encourage your child to sound out the letters in any words he or she does not know. Look at the common "key" words listed at the back of the book and see which of them your child can find on each page.

Check for understanding

It is one thing to understand the meaning of individual words, but you need to make sure that your child understands the facts in the text.

- Play "find the obvious mistake." Read the text as your child looks at the words with you, but make an obvious mistake to see if he or she catches it. Ask your child to correct you and provide the right word.
- After reading the facts, close the book and think up questions to ask your child.
- Ask your child whether a fact is true or false.
- Provide your child with three answers to a question and ask him or her to pick the correct one.

Dictionary and key words

At the end of the book, there is a dictionary page to help your child increase his or her vocabulary. There is also a key words page to reinforce your child's knowledge of the most common words.

DINOSAURS

Amazing dinosaurs lived on our planet many, many years ago. Dinosaurs only lived on land.

Spinosaurus

T. rex

i fact

Dinosaurs were reptiles. Like reptiles today, dinosaurs hatched from eggs.

STEGOSAURUS

STEG-uh-SAWR-us

Stegosaurus was a plant eater. Its body was covered with pointed plates and sharp spikes.

head

(26–30 ft) 8–9 m long
(14 ft) 4.3 m tall

Stegosaurus in the sun

plate

spike

i fact

Some people think the plates on Stegosaurus's back helped it to warm up in the sun.

Stegosaurus had a tiny brain that was about the size of a tangerine!

SPINOSAURUS

SPY-nuh-SAWR-us

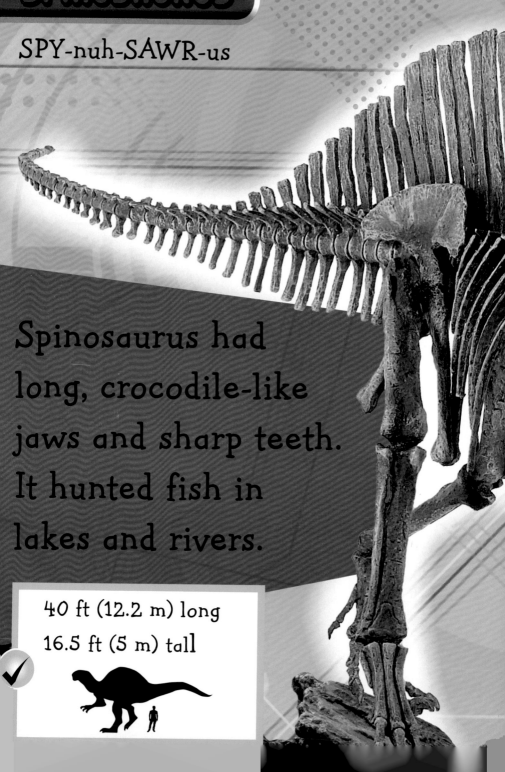

Spinosaurus had long, crocodile-like jaws and sharp teeth. It hunted fish in lakes and rivers.

40 ft (12.2 m) long
16.5 ft (5 m) tall

Spinosaurus's teeth were shaped like cones. This shape was perfect for gripping wriggly fish!

teeth

jaw

13

DIPLODOCUS

Dih-PLOD-uh-kus

Diplodocus was one of the longest-ever animals to walk on land. Its neck could be 26 ft (8 m) long!

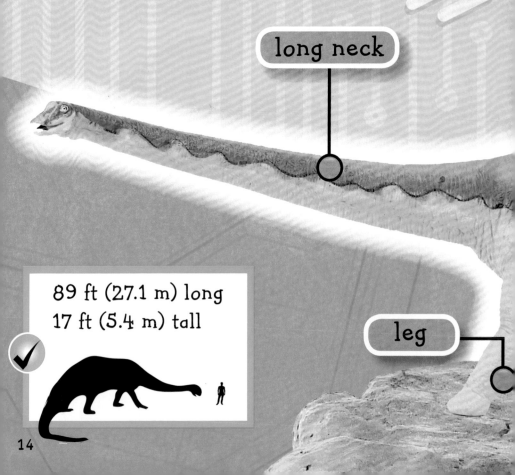

long neck

leg

89 ft (27.1 m) long
17 ft (5.4 m) tall

Diplodocus belonged to a group of dinosaurs called sauropods.

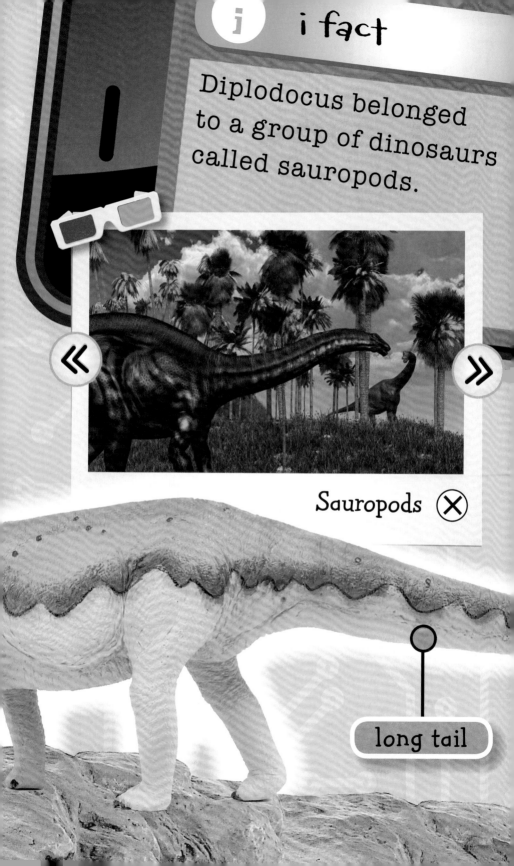

Sauropods ⊗

long tail

T. REX

Tye-RAN-uh-SAWR-us rex

With powerful jaws and pointed teeth, T. rex was a fierce meat eater!

arm

leg

50 ft (15.2 m) long
23 ft (7 m) tall

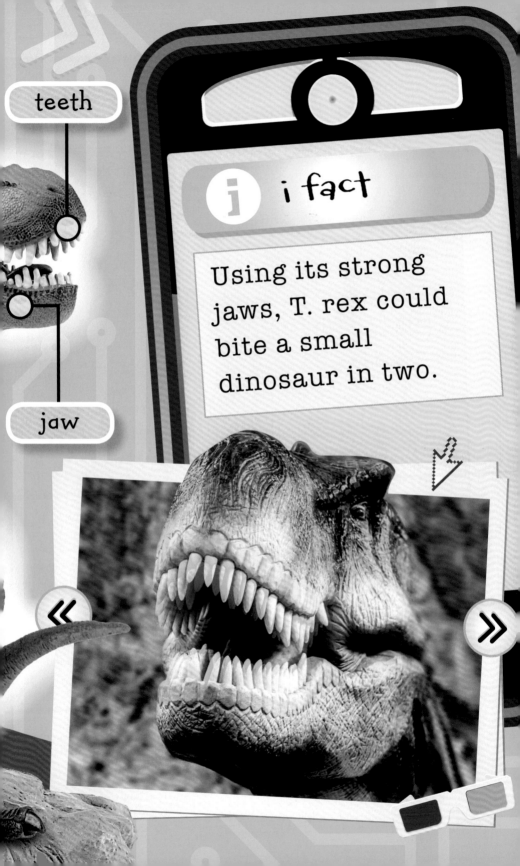

teeth

jaw

j i fact

Using its strong jaws, T. rex could bite a small dinosaur in two.

T. rex had very short arms. Its arms were not even long enough to reach its mouth!

ANKYLOSAURUS

Ang-KILE-uh-SAWR-us

Ankylosaurus could swing its tail club from side to side to break the bones of other dinosaurs.

head

35 ft (10.6 m) long
11 ft (3.4 m) tall

tail

stomach

i fact

Ankylosaurus was a plant eater. It had a large stomach to break down tough plant food.

DEINONYCHUS

Dye-NON-ik-us

Deinonychus was a small, speedy hunter. It used its large toe claws to cut into its prey!

tail

toe claw

9 ft (2.7 m) long
5 ft (1.5 m) tall

teeth

i i fact

Deinonychus and Velociraptor belonged to a group of very smart dinosaurs.

Velociraptor

TRICERATOPS

Try-SAIR-uh-tops

Triceratops had three horns and a large, bony frill sticking out of its huge head.

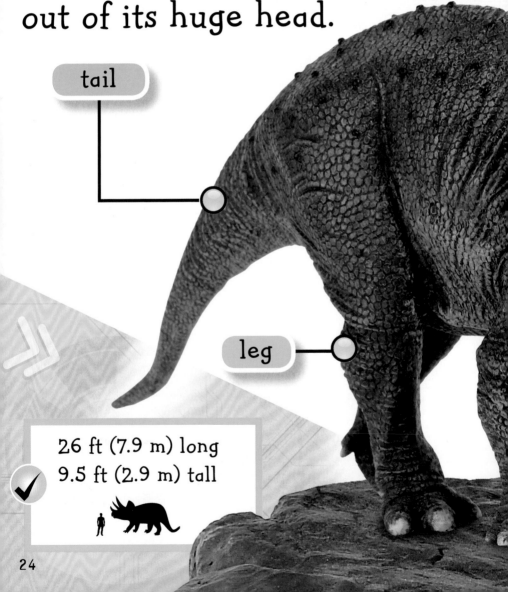

tail

leg

26 ft (7.9 m) long
9.5 ft (2.9 m) tall

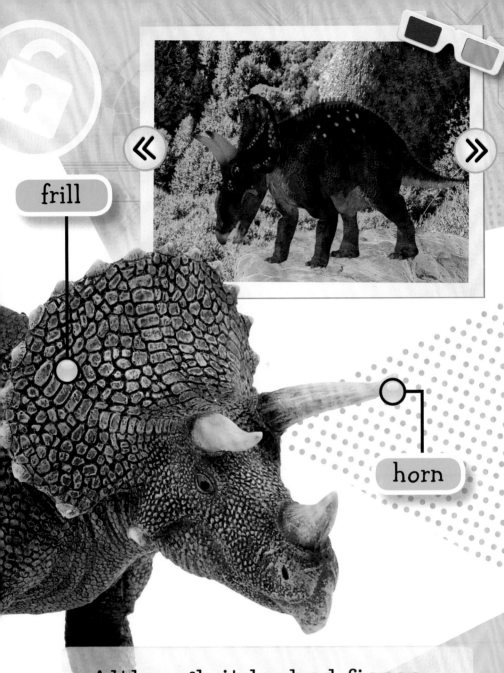

frill

horn

Although it looked fierce, Triceratops only ate plants. It sliced through tough leaves by using strong teeth in its cheeks.

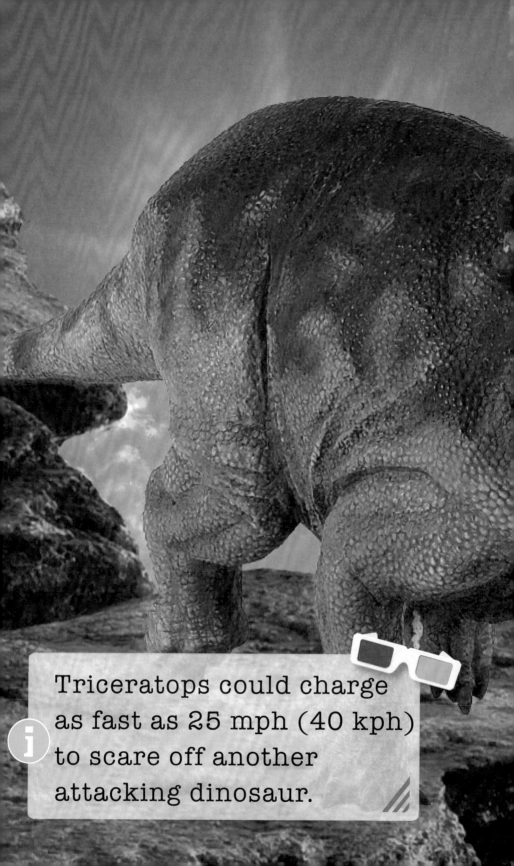

Triceratops could charge as fast as 25 mph (40 kph) to scare off another attacking dinosaur.

The most complete T. rex skeleton is called Sue! It's in a museum in Chicago, Illinois, USA.

Deinonychus's name means "terrible claw."

T. rex skeleton

Spinosaurus had long spines sticking out of its back. We call this a sail.

Stegosaurus stored food in its cheeks just like a hamster.

Ankylosaurus had bony plates on its eyelids!

cone

A cone is a solid shape. It has a round bottom and a pointed top.

fierce

A fierce animal can be wild, strong, and dangerous.

frill

A frill sticks out of an animal's head. Some frills are made from bone.

grip

When you grip something, you hold it tightly.

jaws

Jaws are the parts of the mouth that hold the teeth.

reptile

Most reptiles hatch from an egg. They sit in the sun to warm up and move to the shade to cool down.

wriggly

If something is wriggly, it twists and turns quickly from side to side.

Here are some key words used in context. Help your child to use other words from the border in simple sentences.

Spinosaurus hunted **in** rivers and lakes.

Triceratops had a **big** head.

Deinonychus **was** a smart dinosaur.

The dinosaurs lived on land.

Dinosaurs **all** hatched from eggs.